Seurat

PARK
LANE

"Art is harmony, harmony is the analogy of opposites, the analogy of similar colours, shades and lines."

George Seurat

"In France revolutions are made to safeguard tradition."
Keyserling's words about Georges Seurat effectively sum up the innovatory influence the great painter's work had on all the artists who came after him. It is true that Impressionism was the fuse that set off the artistic revolution which, in the 19th century, managed to break all the sterile links with academic tradition, thus creating the renewal of ideas and inspiration that allowed art to enter new territory and move along previously unknown paths. It is also true, however, that in order to prevent the well running dry, the enthusiastic, young advocates of painting in the open air had, sooner or later, to find a new lifeblood to guarantee the continuity of what they had begun.
In this light the words which Camille Pissarro, the undisputed father of the Impressionist revolution, wrote to his son (also a neo-impressionist painter), on April 1st 1891, take on a great deal of significance: "Yesterday I went to Seurat's funeral and I saw Signac afflicted with grief for this huge loss. I think that you are right when you say that pointillism is finished, but I also think that other things will come out of this technique and that they will be extremely important for the future of art. Seurat has clearly made a big contribution."
The greatness of Seurat is demonstrated by the immense influence he had, not only on the artists of his own generation, but also on those who came after him, at the end of the 19th century and into the 20th. He influenced the 'fauves', the cubists, the futurists and the abstract painters as well as the neo-impressionists. All this he achieved despite his tragically short life.
Georges Seurat was born in Paris on December 2nd, 1859, the third child of a middle-class family which, though not rich, were sufficiently well-off to give their son a classical education. He soon tired of this, however, and enrolled for the art classes given at the local school in Rue des Petits-Hôtels, which proved to be much more to his liking. The relative financial prosperity he enjoyed throughout his life certainly set him apart from some of the other artists of his time who,

Stonecrushers and Other Characters - 1881. Museum of Modern Art, Lillie P. Bliss Collection, New York.

like him, were striving to achieve a long-awaited freedom. What really made him different, however, was his artistic temperament.

After four years at the local school where Seurat studied under Justin Lequien (who was classical in his outlook), Seurat, at nineteen, entered the Ecole des Beaux-Arts, where he studied under Lehmann (a faithful pupil of Ingres). His artistic training is therefore clear: discipline, precision and intensive study of form and composition. For Seurat, however, discipline, precision and formal study were not things imposed on him merely by his academic superiors; they were part of his temperament and his very nature. In some respects the academic atmosphere he found at the Ecole des Beaux-Arts perfectly suited his character, since the precision and discipline that Lehmann tried to impress upon his pupils fully satisfied his own ideals of classical severity and discretion.

Seurat had a great friend in Edmond Aman-Jean whom he had met at the school in Rue des Petits-Hôtels, but he spent most of his time alone visiting art galleries, studying the works of the masters of the distant or more recent past (from Holbein and Raphael to Ingres and Poussin) and, above all, reading: he loved the brothers Goncourt, he studied *La loi du contraste simultané des couleurs* (The Laws of Simultaneous Colour Contrast) by Chevreul and *Grammaire des Arts du dessin* (A Grammar of the Art of Drawing) by Charles Blanc, and he discovered works by N.O. Rood, Humbert de Superville, David Sutter and Charles Henry. He threw himself into the new physical theories of these writers, convinced that mastery of technique was the indispensable basis for any kind of artistic research.

During this same period he copied several paintings by Piero della Francesca. He also visited the fourth exhibition of the Impressionists, and their works had an unforgettable impact on him.

For Seurat, the sight of the Impressionist canvases painted in the open air confirmed the validity of the research he had been carrying out into light, convinced as he was that lines were not the only expressive tool in the hands of the painter.

The late Seventies were a time of great intellectual turmoil of the sort necessary for the birth of new ideas leading to progress in all the different sectors of human knowledge.

Movements such as naturalism, symbolism and positivism — in literature, history, philosophy and science — provided Georges Seurat with plenty of resources on which to draw in his search for his own artistic personality.

1879 was a significant year for Seurat. He left the Ecole des Beaux-Arts and, with two of his friends, Edmond Aman-Jean and Ernest Laurent, set up a studio on the Rue de l'Arbalète: the artistic horizons of Lehmann now appeared too narrow in the eyes of Seurat, although he was never to abandon certain principles which his teacher had instilled in him.

Later that year Seurat had a brief experience which was to be significant for his artistic career: in November he volunteered for the army and was drafted to Brest. Here he discovered the sea, the ideal place to study the phenomenon of changing light.

At the end of his year of military service Seurat returned to Paris with notebooks full of studies and sketches.

Although he liked taking part in heated discussions about art, Seurat was basically quiet and reserved and had a natural tendency to work alone. When he came back to Paris, he opened a studio of his own where he eagerly continued his study of colour in meticulous detail and with scientific precision.

The works he produced during this period, consisting of numerous drawings and also a few paintings, showed the direction in which his research was moving: the drawings were accurately done, with an obvious classical influence with regard to form, and the colours were vibrant and bright, chosen according to optical laws.

Although the luminosity of the Impressionists was a revelation for Seurat, he was unable to accept the apparently temporary nature of their works.

He wanted to investigate the discoveries made by his contemporaries more thoroughly and in greater depth; he refused to reduce artistic experience to something subjectively indeterminate and searched continuously for an 'absolute' method.

Paradoxically, whereas the early Impressionists used optical laws merely to confirm their guiding principle of the abandonment of immediate perception, for Seurat they were one of the basic technical rules which, when assimilated, would give the artist the knowledge and confidence needed to attain complete, conscious freedom of expression.

It was inevitable, therefore, that though he enthusiastically accepted the idea of working in the open air, Seurat spent most of his time in his studio: nature provided him with the tension needed for subsequently working out his precise, complex ideas systematically and painstakingly. During this period Seurat greatly admired Puvis de Chavannes whose work he studied in detail: he even reproduced *Le pauvre pecheur* (The Poor Fisherman) in a sketch that was exhibited at the Salon of 1881. Most of all, however, Seurat was a careful observer of the people around him and their everyday lives, a lesson learnt first from Corot, and then from the Impressionists.

From 1880 to 1884 he made numerous sketches and drawings of everyday subjects: a soldier on a bench, a woman doing her housework, a cat, a man leaning over a parapet, a young girl, a cab driver, his mother sewing, his father eating and many others.

If, on the one hand, however, his choice of subjects shows the attention Seurat paid to the everyday life of which he was part, on the other, the meticulous, repeated execution of sketches and drawings is an evident sign of his fidelity to the principles he was taught at the school in Rue des Petits-Hôtels and the Ecole des Beaux-Arts.

Before taking up his paintbrush, Seurat practised his mastery of the pencil drawing: he studied contrasts, chiaroscuro, light and shade, shading off, vertical lines, horizontal lines and parallel lines, using a simple lead pencil (rarely coloured crayons) or, most frequently of all, a Conté crayon.

In 1882 he visited the sixth Impressionist exhibition, and, in 1883, the seventh. In the same year he presented one of his works to the Jury of the Salon for the first time and won their approval: the work was a life-size, Conté crayon portrait of his friend Aman-Jean.

During the early Eighties, as he perfected his drawing technique, Seurat also began to paint some small canvases in oil. His first attempts clearly show the influence of his academic training, but there is also evidence of real originality with regard to both theme and technique, as in *Fleurs dans un vase* (Flowers in a Vase) and *Baigneuse nue derrière le rideau* (Nude Bather behind the Screen): the strokes are wide, often curved, applied in a helter-skelter fashion and yet are extremely free and fresh. The impression is of a dense, luminous, surprisingly mobile atmosphere.

As time passed, the number of themes Seurat used grew: landscapes and views of Paris, characteristic corners of the city, picturesque alleyways, monumental squares, the famous 'promenades' or the banks of the Seine, sometimes in shadow and sometimes in brilliant sunlight. For each of these paintings, he did several preliminary sketches: he continued to subject himself to the strictest and most scrupulous artistic discipline.

Towards 1882-83 his strokes become shorter and broken and as they gradually take on the characteristic comma shape they appear to approach the typical Impressionist technique. These were years of hard work and painstaking effort, but they were his most productive. By 1883, Seurat's accomplished, mature, artistic personality had emerged. One of the works of this period, which bears witness to the artist's firm belief in the validity of the innovations he was making and also to the scrupulous attention he paid to every detail, is the famous *Une baignade, Asnières* (Bathing at Asnières). This was one of his first large canvases (approximately 2 metres by 3) and was preceded, as always, by a whole series of preliminary studies: drawings and sketches galore, all with infinite variations. Seurat intended to present the canvas to the Salon in 1884 and since 1883, following the example of the Impressionists, he had started to make regular visits to the outskirts of Paris in search of the type of scene or landscape that would give him inspiration.

At Asnières, on the banks of the Seine, he stopped near the village to study the shades of colour on the water, the variations of light in the sky, the landscape and the contrasts of the silhouettes in the river. During his morning walks he filled his notebook with sketches, and then, in the afternoon, he would work on them in the quiet of his studio. His sketches became studies for his painting: a naked back bathed in light, silhouettes moving in the water or stretched out on the grass, dark shadows of trees on the banks or a bright, white sail on the river. The studies are mostly small drawings using Conté crayons but there are also a few in oil. As his study of Asnières deepened and its image became clearer in his mind, Seurat's technique also became clearer and more precise: in the sequence of studies we see his brush or pencil strokes becoming finer and lighter until he achieved the transparency of the colours on the surface of the water or the mobility of the clumps of grass on the river bank that were to be seen in the final version he presented for the approval of the Salon in 1884. A smaller version had already been exhibited in February of the same year at the Cercle des Arts Libres.

The Jury's rejection of the painting, along with those of other young artists, aroused Seurat's indignation and caused the determined reaction which was to bind these artists together in a well-defined group. In protest against the official Salon, all the young painters whose works had been rejected — remembering the similar situation in which the Impressionists had found themselves and which had led to the Salon des Réfusés — founded the Groupe des Artists Indépendants and organized their exhibition as best they could in rooms at the Tuileries.

This marked the beginning of an artistic cooperation which soon bore its first fruits. The regular meetings organized by the Group allowed Seurat to make the acquaintance of other artists worthy of attention, such as Angrand or Dubois-Pillet, as well as writers like Henri de Régnier and Paul Adam. Most importantly, Seurat struck up a personal and professional friendship with Paul Signac, a friendship which was to hold a very important place in both their lives. Together they searched for purity of colour and ways of reproducing nature intact on the canvas, and Signac introduced Seurat to the study of the chromatic analysis of the colours of the prism according to the laws of physics.

The months that followed were months of experimenting together and putting their studies to the test. Although Seurat never abandoned his habit of working alone, he soon moved his studio to Boulevard de Clichy, in a house next to Signac's.

In the following summer, 1885, the first studies and canvases painted using the technique of breaking down colours into their elements finally appeared. They were mostly landscapes, particularly seascapes, inspired by the visit made during the year to Grandcamp. Some of them were painted with extremely short brushstrokes which were often merely a tiny dot of pure colour, the symbol of this new style of painting known as Pointillism, of which Seurat was the undisputed leader.

As a result of his constant critical precision, Seurat had always played

The River Marne at Dawn. Musée Nationale d'Art Moderne, Paris.

an important role within the small group of 'Indépendants'. At their weekly Monday meetings in Signac's house, or at the daily evening meetings in the Café d'Orient or the Café Marengo, Seurat, despite his natural reserve, often played the leading role in creating the new demands and expectations of the young artists.

The group of 'Indépendants' rapidly grew, and in 1885 the already impressive list of names — Redon, Angrand, Dubois-Pillet, Coss, Schuffenecker, Guillaumin — gained that of the famous father of Impressionism, Camille Pissarro, attracted no doubt by the scale of the artistic revolution that Seurat was seeking. In the meantime Seurat was working on the most important of all his large canvases and the one that is generally considered his masterpiece: *Un dimanche après-midi a l'Ile de la Grande Jatte* (Sunday Afternoon on the Isle of Grande Jatte). Started in 1884 and completed in 1886, a first sketch was presented at the exhibition of the 'Indépendants' and the final version was exhibited during the eighth Impressionist exhibition. With the exception of the academics, the work received enthusiastic critical acclaim. As in the other paintings, Seurat's artistic sensibility shows through and here it reaches its most complete expression. "Serious, calm and taciturn" were the words Régnier used to describe Seurat, and, in *La Grande Jatte*, all the human figures portrayed fully reflect this tranquil, solemn image. The scene is one of everyday life and nature, the themes that link Seurat to the Impressionists. The painting depicts the bourgeois habit of indulging in a Sunday promenade along the banks of the Seine, and each of the characters depicted matches the descriptions of Seurat made by his friends. The art critic Gustave Kahn wrote about "the severe regularity of his features" and "the calm look in his eyes" which gave him "a solemn air of austerity", while Degas describes him "walking slowly along the boulevards, correctly dressed, wearing a top hat." The figures in *La Grande Jatte* all seem to move slowly with a correct, measured gait. The only real vivacity in the scene is given by the light and by the clever contrasts and juxtaposition of colours, all achieved through building up a structure with minute points of the brush. The monumental grandeur of the work and its obvious complexity — documented in Seurat's usual manner by a series of 23 drawings and 38 paint sketches — give the canvas such an overwhelming impression of modernity and artistic originality that it became a kind of manifesto of the new artistic movement.

In May and June 1886, the enthusiastic articles written by a certain section of the critics (Fénéon and Verhaeren in particular) mark the official birth of Pointillism, with Seurat as its undisputed leader.

Official recognition did not however change the rhythm or the character of Seurat's research. With his usual critical sense and innate persistence, he went on studying and improving the theories he had formulated, working unceasingly. In the mornings he painted his theme in the open air, and in the afternoon he worked on it further in the solitude of his studio.

The period that followed was a particularly fertile one for Seurat. When he went to Honfleur on the mouth of the Seine in 1886, he found an inexhaustible source of inspiration, painting seven canvases and making numerous studies. From this point on, his pictorial language was based on dots of colour which, as the shades complement and contrast with one another, perfectly capture the light in a skilful play of light and shade.

During the month of September, Seurat's work was again acclaimed during the second 'Indépendant' exhibition, where he exhibited *La Grande Jatte*, several landscapes of Grandcamp and one of his seven most recent pictures, *Coin d'un bassin, Honfleur* (A Corner of the Docks at Honfleur), which the art critic Verhaeren did well to purchase immediately.

In March 1887 when Seurat exhibited his paintings at the third 'Indépendant' exhibition, many of them had already been sold, and critical interest in his work increased even further. This is the period when he painted his most important pictures, from small canvases to large compositions, all preceded and, as it were, 'explained' by an ever increasing number of studies and preliminary drawings. He was so meticulous in his work that Degas nicknamed him 'the notary'. With every new painting Seurat exhibited, he presented all the studies leading to the final composition.

A good example of his meticulous way of working or, as he liked to call it, his 'method', is provided by *Les Poseuses* (Girls Posing), a canvas which, though not finally completed and exhibited until 1888, was preceded by a whole series of sketches, drawings and oil paintings dating back two years. The perfectly balanced composition of the final work shows how the creative work carried out by Seurat enabled him to harmonize each element in the scene despite its obvious complexity. The intensity with which he worked is quite amazing: during the same period that he was working on *Les Poseuses*, Seurat produced, before May 1888, *Parade du Cirque* (Circus Parade), another painting accompanied by a large number of pencil drawings and oil studies. It almost seems as if the way in which he worked so continuously and so tirelessly was somehow meant to compensate for the fact that he would be allowed so little time to devote to his art.

During this fertile period, canvases, drawings and oil paintings on wood followed one another in rapid succession, all with different themes and all with new ideas to propose. A short stay in Port-en-Bessin during the summer of 1888 gave Seurat ideas for six more paintings, all delicate landscapes where the pointillist technique was honed to perfection.

Seurat 'method' became even more conscientious and based on theory. He improved his knowledge of physics, even further by reading and by direct discussions with scientists, and he verified, through his studies, the importance of attentive analysis.

"Art is harmony, harmony is the analogy of opposites, the analogy of similar colours, shades and lines..... The means of expression is the optical synthesis of colours and colour shades or, in other words, of light and its reactions (shade) following the law of contrast, gradation

and irridescence......" This he wrote in 1890 in a letter to Maurice Beaubourg, condensing the significance of all his scientific research and formal innovation in just a few lines.

Meanwhile, his paintings of previous years were crossing national frontiers on their way to an exhibition in Brussels. In 1889 Seurat was working on *Le Chahut*, a painting inspired by a type of dance that was fashionable at the time in the Parisian cafés. It was a new kind of painting for Seurat, because for the first time he had to tackle the problems raised by depicting movement and gaiety. With the same scientific precision he had used to study his delicate, solemn, immobile figures in *Le Chahut*, Seurat put onto canvas an elegant, complex pattern of straight and curved lines conveying an atmosphere of great dynamism and amazing rhythm.

This painting, more than any other, shows the distance between Seurat and the Impressionists: the chromatic separation of pure colours anticipates fauvist techniques, while the search for a geometrically calculated structure teaches the lessons later to be exploited by the cubists.

In the summmer of 1889, during a visit to Le Crotoy, Seurat painted two more canvases and started work on his *Jeune femme se poudrant* (Young Woman Putting on her Make-up). This is a portrait of Madeleine Knoblock whom he had met when she sat for him for *Les Poseuses*, and who gave birth to his son in April, 1890.

The way in which Seurat jealously guarded his fondness for Madeleine, telling only his closest friends about their relationship, fits in perfectly with what we know about his reserved character. In *Jeune femme se poudrant*, the pot of flowers beside the figure of the woman hides the self-portrait which Seurat had originally painted before changing his mind, another example of his personal modesty.

The canvas, which is extremely elegant in composition, was exhibited at the 'Indépendants' exhibition of 1890, together with Seurat's last landscapes and two portraits (of Paul Alexis and Paul Signac).

During that same summer, in addition to the many landscapes inspired by the village of Gravelines, where he stayed for a short while, and La Grenouillère, Seurat found a new source of inspiration in the world of the circus. He made studies of equestriennes, clowns and the circus stalls. He started work on *Le Cirque* (The Circus), his last painting which, although never completed, is, without doubt, one of his most significant from the point of view of the evolution of his technique: the composition is reduced to the bare essentials, and Seurat's quest to find analogies between lines and colours can be clearly sensed.

Although it was incomplete, Seurat decided to exhibit the work at the Salon des Indépendants of March 1891, of which he was in charge. It was his last exhibition. On March 29th 1891, when the exhibition was reaching its climax, Georges Seurat, who was in his thirty-first year, died of the same sudden illness that a fortnight later was to kill his one-year-old son.

In light of his sudden death, the fact that *Le Cirque* was never finished may appear to take on extra significance: an interrupted message that was never fully received. The innovatory content of the work was difficult to grasp at the time, and in fact many critics were quick to say so. But the great distress that was felt throughout the art world when the news of Seurat's death became known gave rise to general recognition of the originality and importance of the discoveries the young artist had made.

Everybody suddenly agreed that Seurat had been the first to realize the 'weaknesses' of the Impressionist movement, and had thus directed his efforts and his research towards finding a strictly scientific basis for his art, while, at the same time, safeguarding the more valid aspects of the Impressionist revolution: this was the important heritage that Georges Seurat left behind for the artists of the 20th century.

1. Flowers in a Vase - 1880 ca. Private collection - *This painting is one of the first oil paintings produced by Seurat. It dates back to the period in which he had just left the academic environment of the School of Fine Arts and had begun to discover Impressionist painting. Here, in fact, the freshness of the composition and the astonishingly free use of brush and colour, reveal the profound impression that Impressionist painting had on the young Seurat.*

2. The Poor Fisherman - 1879-80 ca. Huguette Berès Collection, Paris - *This oil painting on wood seems to summarize Seurat's more mature artistic feelings: the inclusion of a painting by Puvis de Chavannes in a typically Impressionist landscape appears in effect to be an attempt at representing the merging of the classical period with modern naturalism and use of colour.*

3. The Jockey - 1882. Paul Pétridès Collection, Paris - *The silent immobility of this silhouette offers a foretaste of the artist's future paintings, while the short, crossed brushstrokes, although still wide and sweeping, show clear traces of a certain Impressionist influence. The high line of the horizon sets off the image in the foreground and gives a certain depth to the composition.*

4. The Wet Nurse - 1882. Musée du Louvre, Paris - *The mature and accomplished originality of Seurat's art is immediately apparent in his drawings, almost all of which were done in Conté crayon. Using this difficult technique the artist traced his figures with an extraordinary force and, having completely abolished outlines, gave them shape and volume by contrasts of light and shade.*

5. Woman Seated with Crossed Hands - 1881 ca. Morandi Collection, Bologna - *Everyday family life offered numerous ideas for the drawings of Seurat who drew his figures with fresh spontaneity on thick, rather heavy, rough and even granular-textured paper, the irregularity of which was ideal for the chiaroscuro that his pencil strove to achieve on the sheet of paper.*

6. The Gardener - 1882. Private collection, USA - *Although it is one of Seurat's first small-sized oil paintings on canvas, this painting, which is clearly inspired by the themes of the great masters (Corot, Millet) already contains the embryo of one of the basic themes of his paintings: one can in fact observe the original study of the horizontal, vertical and transversal lines in the division of the meadow, in the slender tree on the left and in the stick in the hand of the gardener.*

7. Cab Driver - 1882 ca. Huguette Berès Collection, Paris - *Other ideas for Seurat's drawings were offered, to the attentive eye of the painter, by the details discovered in the streets of Paris. In this drawing, the play of contrasts defines the silhouette of the cab without actually drawing the outlines: the result is spontaneity and originality.*

8. Stonecrusher at Montfermeil - 1882. Private collection, USA - *The theme is taken from a famous picture by Courbet, but Seurat's treatment of it is completely different. The stonecrusher himself is no longer the focal point of the composition: he is captured in the repetitious nature of his work so that he practically becomes part of the countryside. The picture is really about colour contrasts, with the vertical line of the tree on the right acting as a marker of space.*

9. Stonecrusher - 1882. Mellon Collection, Washington, D.C. - *Again Seurat chooses Courbet's stonecrusher as his theme but whereas Courbet was concerned with the worker's social implications Seurat is more interested in him as a point of departure for his research into the effects of light. The wide brushstrokes give an original interpretation of an Impressionist theme.*

10. The Artist's Father at Table - 1884 ca. Private collection, Paris - *The most notable feature of this drawing is the force of expression that Seurat has managed to achieve. The oblique lines give consistency to the figure and give an idea of its volume and weight. The chromatic contrast between the dark bottle in the foreground and the light in the centre of the picture gives movement to the whole scene.*

11. Peasant Girl Sitting on the Grass - 1883. The Solomon R. Guggenheim Collection, New York - *That this canvas is a study of light is obvious and Seurat appears to shorten his brushstrokes in an attempt to create the instantaneous effect given by Impressionist painting. The choice of subject brings to mind Pissarro but the silent grandeur of the figure against the violent background light is a premonition of what Seurat has in store for the future.*

12. Canoe - 1884 ca. Georges Renaud Collection, Paris - *The choice of the theme, the colour scheme, the atmosphere and the technique are all reminiscent of Impressionism but the structural composition, the way in which space is marked by the vertical lines of the trees and the study of the light all bear witness to Georges Seurat's need to create a balanced, ordered, disciplined composition.*

13. Landscape, Ile de France - 1882 Mme. Albert Marquet Collection (legacy to the Musées Nationaux) - *Seurat often took Impressionist open-air themes as his starting-point and then developed the theme according to his own methods of pictorial research. The paintings of these early years therefore have many points of contact with Impressionism even though, for Seurat, this was just a temporary (yet essential) stage in the evolution of his art.*

14. Rue Saint-Vincent in the Snow - 1883. Private collection, USA - *This oil painting on wood is particularly significant with regard to Seurat's research into colour. The luminous atmosphere is heightened by the contrast with the dark touches at the top, which give depth to the whole scene, while the dark, sketchy silhouette and the dark fence on the left and the post on the right provide a frame for the composition and animate the scene.*

15. Horse and Boats, Study for 'Bathing at Asnières' - 1883. Private collection, France - *This is one of the numerous preliminary studies made for the large canvas* Bathing at Asnières *showing the meticulous way in which Seurat carried out his research. The silhouette of the horse against the clear water was included to study colour contrasts and was later eliminated from the work.*

16. Fields of Lucerne at St. Denis - 1885-86. Courtauld Institute Galleries, London - *During this period Seurat was in constant contact with the other artists in the neo-impressionist group and his friendship with Signac was important for the evolution of his use of colour. This canvas is an attempt to break down colours according to the elements of the colour spectrum. The brushstrokes are also shorter and faster.*

17. Street - 1885 ca. Private collection, USA - *The rapid brushstrokes, the roughly sketched shapes and the elegant, incisive composition of this oil painting on wood bear witness to the artistic maturity of Seurat and show how valuable a heritage he left for future painters. The immediate way in which the freshness and vitality of this street is rendered anticipates future, abstract trends in painting.*

18. The Bridge at Courbevoie, Study for 'Bathing at Asnières' - 1883-84. Enriques Collection - *This oil-painting on wood is another of the many preparatory studies made for* Bathing at Asnières *and is basically a study of one detail of the scene. All the preliminary sketches, particularly this one, have richer, brighter colours than the final version.*

19. Bathing at Asnières - 1883-84. The Tate Gallery, London - *This is Seurat's first large canvas and was exhibited during the first exhibition of the 'Indépendants'. The theme and the place are typically impressionistic, but the technique and the composition anticipate the classical solemnity and diffused luminosity of Georges Seurat's later works.*

20. Le Bec du Hoc, Grandcamp - 1885. The Tate Gallery, London - *The impression of dramatic solemnity given by the rock standing alone in the centre of this picture is heightened by the sensation of infinite space and the immensity of the sea. Short strokes and dots of colour give the impression of distant sails and the flight of birds adds a vibrant effect to the atmosphere.*

21. The Coast at Bas-Butin, Honfleur - 1886. Musée des Beaux-Arts, Tournai - *This is one of the seven pictures Seurat painted at Honfleur in 1886. The landscape at Honfleur provided the starting point for experiments regarding composition and research into colour. The simplicity of the structure, based on very few elements, and the clearly pointillist technique give a calm, balanced impression in an atmosphere of diffused light.*

22. Final Study for 'La Grande Jatte' - 1884-85. The Metropolitan Museum of Art, New York - *This is the final study Seurat made for his masterpiece and it already contains all the elements to be found in the final version. The vibration of light and colour, the triumphant effects of light and the natural freshness of the composition put this study almost on the same level as the final version, which is more mature and more precise.*

23. Sunday Afternoon on the Isle of Grande Jatte - 1884-86. The Art Institute of Chicago - *This work is such a complete expression of Seurat's artistic maturity that it has become a kind of manifesto of his artistic beliefs. It represents the triumph of Pointillism, of which Seurat was the undisputed master. No traces of the hard labour and meticulous research that went into the creation of the work can be seen in the final version.*

24. Study for 'Gravelines, One Evening' - 1890. Musée de l'Annonciade, Saint Tropez - *The canal at Gravelines was often painted by Seurat who found an ideal subject for his research into colour in its rarefied atmosphere and the variations of colour and light on the surface of the water. This study is an interesting and unusual example of the pointillist technique.*

25. A Corner of the Docks at Honfleur - 1886. Kröller-Müller Stichting, Otterlo - *The spontaneity of this work, which in fact derives from a long study of colour decomposition and chromatic combinations, made it a great success at the exhibition of the 'Indépendants' in 1886. The skilful use of vertical, horizontal and slanting lines bears witness to the complexity of the composition.*

26. Standing Nude, Study for 'Girls Posing' - 1886-87. Georges Renaud Collection, Paris - *The academic theme of the female nude was tackled by Seurat with an originality and modernity that belied the critics who said that pointillism was a limited technique. The free, almost approximative technique used, with short, crossed brushstrokes, gives lightness to the image.*

27. Girls Posing (small version) - 1888. Berggruen Collection, Paris - *This is a small version painted after the larger one to be seen at the Barnes Foundation Collection at Merion in Pennsylvania. The precise, calculated solidity of the formal composition harmonizes well with the intimacy and fragility of the figures who appear to be more spontaneous in this version than in the larger, more meticulously planned original.*

28. Seated Nude, Back View, Study for 'Girls Posing' - 1886-87. Musée du Louvre, Paris - *Unanimously considered by the critics to be the best of all the studies for* Girls Posing, *this oil painting on wood shows the maturity which Seurat had brought to the pointillist technique. The silhouette is gently modelled by the dots of colour and no outline is drawn. The atmosphere is created by a skilful use of light and shade.*

29. Seated Nude, Profile, Study for 'Girls Posing' - 1886-87. Musée du Louvre, Paris - *Less elegant and less subtle than the previous one, this study is nevertheless significant because of its modern approach to colour. The dark zones contrast with the lighter ones to define the volumes while the contrast between the brown hair and the light background creates a halo of light around the girl's face.*

30. The Singer of the Eden Concert Hall - 1887-88. Stedelijk Museum Collection, Amsterdam - *As in various other paintings, the choice of theme, the point of view and the presence of certain details seem to suggest an Impressionist approach. The double bass, for example, reminds one of Degas. The atmosphere of diffused light, however, and the meticulous technique used are typical of Seurat.*

31. Singer of 'La Gaité' Café, Rochechouart - 1887-88. Rhode Island School of Design, Museum of Art, Providence - *Particularly significant in terms of Seurat's research into natural and artificial light, the works with indoor scenes show that Georges Seurat adopted different criteria from those he used when painting outdoor scenes. The atmosphere is nevertheless one of diffused light.*

32. Grey Skies at Grande Jatte - 1888. Private collection, USA - *The Isle of Grande Jatte was an inexhaustible source of inspiration for Seurat, and he painted it on many occasions and at different times of the day and year. The essentially static composition of this picture is brought alive by the vibration of the light and the pointillist technique used.*

33. The Seine at Grande Jatte in Springtime - 1888. Musées Royaux des Beaux-Arts de Belgique, Brussels - *More mobile than the previous painting, where the composition is the same but back to front, this canvas shows the delicacy of Seurat's pictorial technique. The one point of pure colour allows the artist to bathe the whole scene in a luminous, crystalline atmosphere.*

34. Corner of the Artist's Studio, Study for 'Girls Posing' - 1886-87. Musée du Louvre, Paris - *Although conceived merely as a detail to be inserted into the large canvas Girls Posing, this drawing shows Seurat's brilliant technique as well as bearing witness to the methodical way in which he planned his works.*

35. Sunday, Port-en-Bessin - 1888. Kröller-Müller Stichting, Otterlo - *The structure of this canvas reveals a carefully studied, geometrical composition which almost gives the impression of being cold and too severe. The artist's sensibility, however, brings the scene to life by the use of warm colours and by the lighter touch of the flags flying in the wind.*

36. Study for 'Circus Parade' - 1887. Stiftung Samm-lun Emil G. Bührle, Zurich - *Half way between a fan-tastic vision and a solemn ceremony, this study shows incredible freedom of chromatic expression. The bold use of violet, green and orange gives this study a vivacity and a mobility that are lost in the final version.*

37. Study for 'Circus Parade' - 1887. Private Collec-tion, Basel - *An unusual example of a pen and ink drawing, this study is the same as the final version which was completed the following year, except for a few small details: the tree on the left of the final version is missing and a few minor details of the figures in the au-dience are different.*

38. Circus Parade - 1887-88. The Metropolitan Mu-seum of Art, legacy of Stephen C. Clark, New York - *The geometrical structure of this work, its abstraction and its enigmatic symbolism make it a precursor of twentieth-century art. The rhythmical sequence of verti-cal lines creates a curiously disturbing atmosphere.*

39. The Circus - 1890-91. Musée d'Orsay, Paris - *Cle-verly structured and architecturally balanced, this was Seurat's last painting and it was never finished. Despite the laborious preliminary work which, as usual, preceded the final version, the freshness of the subject remains in-tact. The warm, almost unreal, light gives the impres-sion of something fantastic and the repetition of ascend-ing lines give vivacity and movement to the scene.*

40. Study for 'The Circus' - 1890. Musée du Louvre, Paris - *This preliminary study is a good example of the meticulous research carried out by Seurat for his final canvas: it shows an analysis of the ascending lines which are used to give structure to the whole composi-tion, like a basic architectural element in perfect harmony.*

41. Study for 'Le Chahut' - 1889-90. Courtauld Institute Galleries, London - *This is the first sketch made for the canvas which is now to be found in Otterlo. The world of entertainment was a favourite subject of the artists of the period. Seurat, however, gives a very personal interpretation of the theme. It was the first time he had tackled the problem of fast movement and enjoyment contrasting the solemn immobility of his previous compositions.*

42. Le Chahut - 1889-90. Kröller-Müller Stichting, Otterlo - *In a precise composition of ascending curves, Seurat celebrates the triumph of movement and gaiety, achieved by means of sophisticated details. Despite the obvious complexity of the structural composition, one can sense a freshness of invention and a hidden touch of irony in the odd faces of the dancers and the bizarre nature of certain details and gestures.*

43. Portrait of Paul Signac - 1889. Private collection, Paris - *In this drawing it is possible to sense the friendship that existed between Signac and Seurat. Signac is seen in profile, with a serious look on his face and yet the perfect balance of the composition and the harmony of the lines and the chiaroscuro make the overall effect one of great serenity.*

44. Young Woman Putting on her Make-up - 1889-90. Courtauld Institute Galleries, London - *The composition of this work is extremely complex and the technique particularly refined. The immobile figure of the woman emerges against a background of powdery matter; she is captured in a moment of intimacy, out of time.*

1. *Flowers in a Vase* - 1880 ca. Private collection.

2. *The Poor Fisherman* - 1879-80 ca. Huguette Berès Collection, Paris.

3. *The Jockey* - 1882. Paul Pétridès Collection, Paris.

4. *The Wet Nurse* - 1882. Musée du Louvre, Paris.

5. *Woman Seated with Crossed Hands* - 1881 ca. Morandi Collection, Bologne.

6. *The Gardener* - 1882. Private collection, USA.

7. *Cab Driver* - 1882 ca. Huguette Berès Collection, Paris.

8. *Stonecrusher at Montfermeil* - 1882. Private collection, USA.

9. *Stonecrusher* - 1882. Mellon Collection, Washington, D.C.

10. *The Artist's Father at Table* - 1884 ca. Private collection, Paris.

11. *Peasant Girl Sitting on the Grass* - 1883. The Solomon R. Guggenheim Collection, New York.

12. *Canoe* - 1884 ca. Georges Renaud Collection, Paris,

13. *Landscape, Ile de France* - 1882 Mme. Albert Marquet Collection (legacy to the Musées Nationaux)

14. *Rue Saint-Vincent in the Snow* - 1883. Private collection, USA.

15. *Horse and Boats, Study for 'Bathing at Asnières'* - 1883. Private collection, France.

16. *Fields of Lucerne at St. Denis* - 1885-86. Courtauld Institute Galleries, London.

17. *Street* - 1885 ca. Private collection, USA.

18. *The Bridge at Courbevoie, Study for "Bathing at Asnières"* - 1883-84.
Enriques Collection.

19. *Bathing at Asnières* - 1883-84. The Tate Gallery, London.

20. *Le Bec du Hoc, Grandcamp* - 1885.
   The Tate Gallery, London.

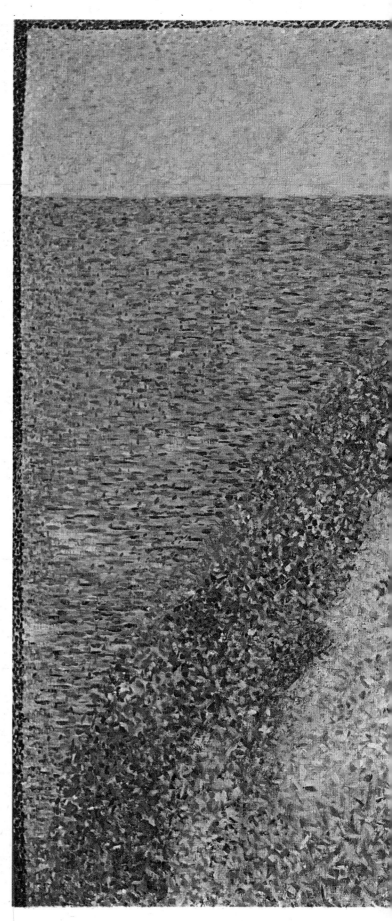

21. *The Coast at Bas-Butin, Honfleur* - 1886. Musée des Beaux-Arts, Tournai.

22. *Final Study for 'La Grande Jatte'* - 1884-85.
The Metropolitan Museum of Art, New York.

23. *Sunday Afternoon on the Isle of Grande Jatte* - 1884-86.
The Art Institute of Chicago.

24. *Study for 'Gravelines, One Evening'* - 1890. Musée de l'Annonciade, Saint Tropez.

25. *A Corner of the Docks at Honfleur* - 1886. Kröller-Müller Stichting, Otterlo.

26. *Standing Nude, Study for 'Girls Posing'* - 1886-87.
Georges Renaud Collection, Paris.

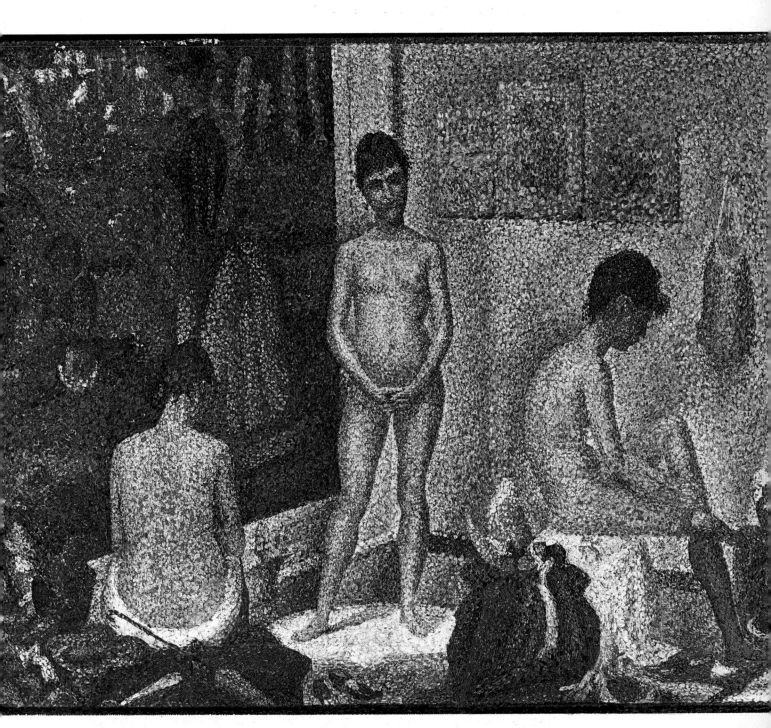

27. *Girls Posing (small version)* - 1888. Berggruen Collection, Paris.

28. *Seated Nude, Back View, Study for 'Girls Posing'* -
1886- 87. Musée du Louvre, Paris.

29. *Seated Nude, Profile, Study for 'Girls Posing'* -
1886-87. Musée du Louvre, Paris.

30. *The Singer of the Eden Concert Hall* - 1887-88. Stedelijk Museum Collection, Amsterdam.

31. *Singer of 'La Gaité' Café, Rochechouart - 1887-88.*
Rhode Island School of Design, Museum of Art, Providence.

32. *Grey Skies at Grande Jatte* - 1888. Private Collection, USA.

33. *The Seine at Grande Jatte in Springtime* - 1888. Musées Royaux des Beaux-Arts de Belgique, Brussels.

34. *Corner of the Artist's Studio, Study for 'Girls Posing'* - 1886-87. Musée du Louvre, Paris.

35. *Sunday, Port-en-Bessin* - 1888. Kröller-Müller Stichting, Otterlo.

36. *Study for 'Circus Parade'* - 1887. Stiftung Sammlung Emil G. Bührle, Zurich.

37. *Study for 'Circus Parade'* - 1887. Private Collection, Basel.

38. *Circus Parade* - 1887-88. The Metropolitan Museum of Art,
legacy of Stephen C. Clark, New York.

40. *Study for 'The Circus'* - 1890. Musée du Louvre, Paris.

39. *The Circus* - 1890-91. Musée d'Orsay, Paris.

41. *Study for 'Le Chahut'* - 1889-90. Courtauld Institute Galleries, London.

42. *Le Chahut* - 1889-90. Kröller-Müller Stichting, Otterlo.

43. *Portrait of Paul Signac* - 1889. Private collection, Paris.

44. *Young Woman Putting on her Make-up* - 1889-90. Courtauld Institute Galleries, London.

Editor in chief Anna Maria Mascheroni

Art director Luciano Raimondi

Text Alberta Melanotte

Translation Kerry Milis

Production Art, Bologna

Photo Credits Gruppo Editoriale Fabbri S.p.A., Milan

Copyright © 1988 by Gruppo Editoriale S.p.A., Milan

Published by Park Lane
An imprint of Books & Toys Limited
The Grange
Grange Yard
LONDON
SE1 3AG

ISBN 1-85627-101-3

This edition published 1991

Printed in Italy by Gruppo Editoriale Fabbri S.p.A., Milan